P9-CEQ-385

NOW
Breathe

Now Breathe

A Journal of Life after a Cancer Diagnosis

Claudia Sternbach

WHITEAKER PRESS

Now Breathe: A Journal of Life after a Cancer Diagnosis

Library of Congress Cataloging-in-Publication Data

Sternbach, Claudia
Now breathe: a very personal journal of breast cancer / Claudia Sternbach -- 1st ed.
p. cm.
LCCN: 98-83286
ISBN 0-9653800-4-1

1. Sternbach, Claudia--Health. 2. Breast--Cancer--Patients--United States--Biography.
I. Title

RC280.B8S747 1999
362.1/9699449/0092 [B] QB199-107

Published in the United States of America by
Whiteaker Press
204 First Avenue South, Suite 3
Seattle, Washington 98104

Dedicated to

Kira and Michael,
my sun and moon

Thank you

Thank you to the women in my writing group, Kathryn Chetkovich, Frances Hatfield, Candida Lawrence, Joan McMillan, Maude Meehan, Amber Coverdale Sumrall, Dena Taylor, Ellen Treen and Sherrie Tucker. Your constant support has been invaluable.

Thanks to my teachers, Anne Lamott and Adair Lara, who reminded me to look for the angle, find the hook, and take it bird by bird.

To Cathryn Alpert and Nora Boothby, experts at editing.

To Claud Mauro for taking a chance.

And to all my friends and family. Not only are your names written in these pages, they are inscribed upon my heart.

CONTENTS

. . . eighty-two days.

NOW
Breathe

• SUNDAY NIGHT, DECEMBER 18

Got home from a beautiful family dinner at my sister's house. Kira spending the night with Katy. Settle into bed to watch a Woody Allen movie. Bored by the movie. I like "Woody in New York" movies. This is too slapstick for me. Raise my right arm over my head and begin to do a breast exam. Woody can be so good. Why did he make this movie? Find a lump. Not unusual. But this lump feels different to me. Hard. Make a mental note to call for checkup in the morning. Know it will be nothing. Good to check though. Stop watching the movie halfway through. Sleep hard.

• Monday, December 19

First day of Christmas vacation. Call doc. Eleven-thirty appointment. Perfect. I can pick Kira up at Katy's, take her to piano her lesson and go to the doctor from there. Perfect timing. We'll be home by noon.

Leave Kira in the waiting room. Tell her I'll only be a few minutes. She knows why we are here. But she knows it is no big deal.

Red flag. Doc wants to send me for mammogram right now. Calls radiation himself. Says I'm on my way over. Just across the parking lot. Just playing it safe.

Kira and I hold hands as we walk. She's nine. Knows the truth about a lot of things. I tell her it's nothing. I tell her that's the truth. Again I leave her in the waiting room.

As I head to my cubicle to put on my "open down the front please robe" I stop and use the phone. Call my friend Nora. Please come get Kira. Something is happening here. I can't have her here. I can't have her see my fear.

Sitting in my cubicle. Curtain open. A woman walks by. I know her. She is a parent of a friend of Kira's. A therapist. Seems she snores. Driving her family nuts. Having some x-rays. Seeing if peace can be restored.

Mammogram doesn't show much. Try ultrasound. I meet the monster in the closet. There it is on the screen in front of me. A perfectly round ball. A cat's-eye marble. A full moon. My third eye. I attempt to stare it down. I blink first.

It's probably nothing. But let's call a surgeon. It should really come out. It's probably nothing. But let's take it out.

Go home. Call Michael at work. Try to be cool. Don't know what I said. Call Nora. Get Kira. Tell her what is going on. She cries. Accuses me of lying to her. Says she knows I'm going to die. Like my friend a few weeks ago. I tell her that's not true. I am fine. She may open a Christmas present if she wants. Mini table-tennis. Suction cups stick to the table to hold up the tiny net. She's smiling again. We go to the grocery store. I am calm on the outside. I am a hurricane inside. I can remove potato chips from the shelf. I can plan a Christmas party for my Tuesday writing class. I remember to buy vanilla ice cream. Madeline is allergic to chocolate.

But I buy nothing for dinner. And my hands are very cold.

• Tuesday, December 20

I have a four o'clock appointment with the surgeon. It is the only time he has. My writing class is 3:30 to 5:00. Won't cancel. Kids are exchanging gifts. Wrapping their holiday projects.

Call my friend Chris. Explain what is going on. Kira is watching my every move. Listening to the tone of my voice. Looking for signs. Anger and fear mixed. Chris is coming. I won't be gone long. I swear. I stay until most of the kids arrive. Explaining to them all why I need to leave. I will be back before class is over.

I like driving the Trooper. It is big and makes me feel powerful. There is something to this thing some guys have with cars. I enjoy parking in the doc's parking lot and feeling taller than everyone around me. I take pleasure in the feel of it's heavy door. I slam it.

His name is Doctor S. I like him. We dispense with those stupid robes. Take off your shirt. Let me see the lump. I don't think it's cancer. But it needs to come out. He can say the word cancer. Right to my face. He can look me in the eye when he says it. And he knows that the robes are an absurd detail when talking about mutant cells.

We'll do the surgery in the morning. I tuck in my shirt while we talk. I am able to do this without unbuttoning my jeans. I have lost weight and my jeans are loose. It is the first time I really notice.

I get home before class is over. The kids open gifts. Michael comes home. We turn on the tree lights. It is almost normal. I notice how many sphere-shaped objects there are around me. My daughter's big blue eyes.

My friend Julie arrives to pick up her daughters. I tell her I need a favor. She knows what is going on already. She had called me on her car phone. We plan for Kira to spend the next day at her house. We'll drop her off on the way to surgery.

Michael calls work to tell them he won't be in. Seems strange to have him here on a weekday morning. Special. Like a vacation. Wish we were going out to breakfast.

Drive up to Julie's house. Michael clocks it from the turn. Two point six miles to the mailbox. We drive up through the apple orchard. Winter-bare tree limbs. Arms reaching. The barn at the top of the hill. Through the window I see the kids at the table eating breakfast. Robert is the cook. This is a good place for Kira to spend the day. I call out good-bye and we're off.

The sun is bright. My eyes feel very sensitive. Michael remembered to bring the newspaper with us. We check in. But there is no time for me to read Herb Caen. I know people here. They will take good care of me. I am having a local. I'll be awake. No surprises. I have to undress. Another stupid gown. I am wrapped in warm blankets. I get a blue cap to wear. Everyone is wearing them. I am a member of the club. We need a new uniform. It brings out the blue in my eyes, I am told, when I complain about the look. Sylvia, the nurse, holds my hand while the I.V. is done. I am given a plastic bottle filled with warm water to hold. It will help warm my hands. Booties are put on my feet. I am wheeled into surgery. Draped.

The clock is on the wall. I make a note to try to keep track of the time. I chat with Sylvia. My arms are stretched out on two boards. Sylvia makes a reference to Jesus on the cross. Wrong holiday,

I tell her. I wish for a headset and television. I would like to watch *Beetlejuice,* I reply when asked what movie I would choose.

I have forgotten to watch the clock. The lump is out. Doctor S. says it looks okay. I tell him I want to see it. He doesn't hesitate. There it is. In his hand. Reminds me of when my mother-in-law cleans out the turkey at Thanksgiving. It's not beautiful. It is no longer round. I get to go home now.

We should know by tomorrow.

Michael is gentle with me in the car.

At three-thirty my Wednesday writing class arrives. I stay on the couch. I explain why. They finish their projects and wrap them. They exchange gifts and play Christmas music on their instruments. At five they all leave and Michael goes to get Kira. He even takes Moka. Doesn't want me to be pummeled by the dog while he's gone.

I am functioning.

At seven-thirty Michael and Kira join friends for Christmas caroling in the neighborhood. They come and stand in front of our house. I go out and sit on the porch swing. They sound like angels. There is a half moon. Kira comes and sits with me. Katy joins us. Then Kaitlin. Lauren. The Christmas lights up the hill at Sue's house are beautiful. The streetlight illuminates the singers. Even Ed is there. Singing. I'm tired but I feel good. Peaceful. None of these people will let anything bad happen to me. And I won't either.

• Thursday, December 22

Michael is off to work. But he makes me coffee first. And brings in the paper. And puts the cereal where I can reach it. I can't lift my right arm. Kira gets up and dressed. Fixes me cereal. Pours me coffee. Hugs me. Soft., like I might break. Becky comes to pick her up. They are going off for a day at the beach. Movies. Burger King. A kid's day. I try not to watch the clock. Stare at the phone. I remember what Doc S. said. It looks good.

At eleven I call. Call back after two she says. Two forty-five. Try after four. Four-thirty. Tomorrow for sure. Oprah has a cooking show on. The no-fat french fries look really good. I'm pissed. I call Michael just to hear him. So that I can leave the place I have been living in all day and re-enter his world. Like a space walker on a tether. I want him to reel me in.

The phone rings every three minutes. It's okay. It's like being in labor. Waiting.

I have trouble sleeping.

• Friday, December 23

Michael leaves the house a bit after six. Kira is home with me today. We are going to go with some friends to the movies later. Yesterday was spent in limbo. Enough of that. I am back in charge again.

Eight a.m. I make my first call. Nine-thirty. Ten o'clock. Ten-thirty. Eleven-fifteen. The results are in. I hear a note of annoyance in the receptionist's voice.

Doctor S. comes on the line. His voice is a soothing gray blue. He says I have cancer. I am calm. Kira and her friend Erica are standing by me. They are showing me "cat's cradle." I am trying to watch while listening to the doctor. My heart seems to be beating out a new rhythm. C,A,N,C,E,R. He gives me his home number. He says he will be with me for the whole race. Unless I get sick of him. He will see Michael and me on Tuesday morning. More surgery next week. He says I can call him. I hang on to that. I hang up the phone.

The girls are off playing. I take the phone out to the garage. I call Michael at work. I try not to cry. But there is a howl locked in my throat. It will have to come out sometime. I say the word myself. For the first time. It has become my word. I own it now. I whisper it to Michael and feel his face go pale. He's coming right home. I worry about his driving. I call my friend Nora. Erica's mother. I call my own mother. I put myself in her place. Could I bear to hear these words from my own child? I tell her I'm sorry. I really mean it. I hang up and let myself cry for just a minute. No noise. Then I go in to talk to Kira.

She sits on my lap in my father's old leather chair. Erica stands close by. That's okay with me. Keep things as normal as possible. We are going to fix this, I tell her. She cries. I try to gather her closer to me. Her legs are long. She is almost as big as me. But her face is like a baby's. Skin so soft.

I offer her another present.

Kids are kids. It helps. By the time Michael gets home Kira and Erica are sorting her new hockey cards and placing them in the album.

I make a few more phone calls. There needs to be a book of rules written. Just exactly what am I supposed to do? I'm flying by the seat of my pants.

I try to call my friend Becky. Her mother is there. She is crying. The news has traveled fast. Becky is already on her way over. I meet her in the driveway. She wraps her arms around me. We cry. Out there. Where anyone driving by might see. Nora joins us. I have never been more aware of being a woman. Michael watches us from the yard. He looks so alone.

I drive down the hill to the store. I buy a sequined dress to wear to a Christmas party that night. I have a conversation with the clerk. I can write out a check. I drive back home.

Our friends arrive. We go to the movies. *Dumb and Dumber.* It really is. I am able to make a joke. This movie makes the conversation with the doctor seem funny. Kira treats me to candy. She insists. But she buys her favorite kind. I like that. She knows there is a problem. But she doesn't think I'm going to die. When we get home she makes me pudding. Chocolate. She makes me a bubble bath.

Michael puts clean flannel sheets on the bed. He tops it with my favorite quilt.

I put on my new dress. It picks up the reflection of the lights on the tree. I wear high heels. Black stockings. Makeup.

We go to the party. Michael, Kira and I.

No one can see them yet. But I have put on the gloves. Everlast gloves. And Michael has laced them. And Kira has kissed them. For luck. And that monster in the closet had better duck. He'll never know what hit him.

And I will float. Like a butterfly.

Sting. Like a bee.

• Saturday, December 24

Bow out of entertaining tonight at our house. At the last minute accept an invitation from some good friends to spend the evening at their house. Fire in the fireplace. Cracked crab. Good wine. We are an interesting group. One couple with a three-week-old baby. Still in that blissful haze brought on by sweet baby smells and noises. And sleep deprivation. Another couple who have separated, but are together for the holiday. For the children? Michael and Kira and I. Together because we wouldn't want to be anywhere else.

We sit around the dining room table. A ten-foot tree sits in the corner. Music is playing. The new father holds his daughter. Nuzzling her neck. He knows that no harm can ever come to her. Not while he is there to protect her. He offers to let me hold her. He doesn't know. I wonder, for just an instant, if he would make the same offer if he did know. Would I? Rational thinking plays no part in this. I feel contaminated. But I take her. And hold her against my breast. And breathe in her perfection.

• Sunday, December 25

Michael and I are awake before Kira. We check the stockings to make sure nothing was forgotten. I put on some Christmas music. Kira wakes up and comes to me before checking out her loot.

Wants me to open a gift first. A beautiful book about Jackie Kennedy. I fall apart. We all do. We are huddled together on the couch. Looking for protection from the storm. And then it passes. Our gifts are opened slowly. We taste each moment.

Replace the Christmas music with a new Melissa Etheridge tape. I am tired of the sounds of Christmas. I want music with an edge to it. Hard driving music. Sung by a woman who sounds in control.

Neighbors drop in. We have coffee and cinnamon rolls. Roller blades are tried out in the garage.

Gathering up the gifts for my family, we pack up the car. We are heading over the hill to my mother's house to spend the day. It will be the first time we have seen them all since the news. I know that they will be watching me. Looking for clues. Looking to see how I act. So they can react.

Blast Melissa E. in the car. As we pass other drivers I play a game—can I spot the ones with cancer. If my eyes meet theirs will there be a spark of recognition?

At my mother's I have trouble looking anyone in the eye. There is something in the room with us that is foreign. An intruder. And it is my fault. I brought the stranger to dinner. It changes everything. A joke is made about me being the only one in the family who doesn't eat red meat. That maybe I should have.

In bed that night I feel as if I have run back-to-back marathons. Michael and I are both exhausted. But we have accomplished something amazing. We pulled off Christmas.

• Monday, December 26

I need to get out early. There is something I do every year. The day after Christmas I go out searching for the perfect glass snowball to buy for Kira. It is her first gift for next year. They are expensive. The really special ones. The ones that play beautiful music. But today they are half-off. See, I can still be practical.

The music box store is crowded. I can't decide which one to get. I wind them up. One. Two. Three at a time. "Jingle Bell Rock" is overlapping "Silent Night." "White Christmas" is bringing up the rear.

One snowball catches my eye. In it there is an angel. She is wrapped in a quilt. A quilt that looks as though it were taken from my collection. Her hair is blond. The same color mine used to be. I pick it up and hold it in my hands. I turn it upside down and watch the snow flurries. It plays "I'll Be Home for Christmas." I imagine Kira opening it next year. Kira and Michael. And I'm not there. And I put it back on the shelf and wish it were physically possible to kick myself in the ass.

Teddy bears dancing to "Rock Around the Clock" will be opened next year.

• Tuesday, December 27

Appointment with the surgeon this morning. Need to set up the next operation. Got to check out the lymph nodes. See if they are in the game or not. Michael is taking the morning off to go along. To help me listen to every word the doctor says, to help me sort it out later. I take along a notebook to write everything down.

Becky picks up Kira to spend the day. What would I do without my friends?

She is out the door with a backpack full of who knows what. Hardly a backward glance. This is good. This is normal. But I wanted a hug.

There is another couple in the doc's waiting room. They are sitting close together, her arm curled through his. She is leaning against his chest. Tears are streaming down her face. Water spots forming on her pink leggings. He is sleeping. Head resting against the wall. I assume they have had more than one sleepless night lately. Discussing their fears in the darkness. She gets up to go to the bathroom. He wakes for an instant. Then escapes once more. Soft snores.

She returns and they are taken in to see Doc. S. The door closes behind them. My palms sweat for her.

And then they're back. And she is smiling. Even makes a small joke about the princess and the pea. I fill in the blanks. Her cancer is the size of a pea. And she, the princess, has found it. Felt it herself.

And it must be removed. So the princess can sleep once more.

Doctor S. is good.

We sit across from him in his office. He has to go out of town for a few days and if I want I can wait until he returns to have the next surgery. I don't want to wait. I have a fear of heights, I tell him. And this is like knowing that I have to go off the high dive sometime next week. The anticipation is worse than the actual jump. I want to get it over with.

How about today, he says. What did you eat for breakfast? What time? I'll call the hospital right now. They have a bed. Go right from here. I'll see you in surgery. It will all be fine.

And then I'm in bed. Blood has been taken. Michael has gone home to get me all the things I think I might need for the next twenty-four hours.

Once again I am wearing nothing but a thin cotton gown. It opens down the back and was impossible for me to fasten. I have been wrapped in blankets and have had cotton bootie-like socks put on my feet. But I am freezing. And I am beginning to notice a pattern. In this position I feel vulnerable. Helpless. And it is almost impossible to keep from crying. In fact I start to. And the nurse pretends not to notice. I think of my friend who died of breast cancer. I think of how many times she had to lie in a bed just like this. Wrapped in blankets. Still cold. And wait for someone to make her better. And how no matter how hard everyone tried, nothing worked. And I wonder if nothing works for me, will I see her again. And in an odd way that comforts me.

Michael comes back. We hold hands and watch television. But there is nothing on at two in the afternoon. I channel-surf.

And then it's time. Michael walks alongside as my bed is wheeled down to surgery. Just outside the double doors he is told he may go no further. He kisses my forehead and strokes my head. He tells me he'll be waiting. No matter what, he'll be waiting.

My chest feels tight and my throat hurts from trying not to cry. I am wheeled through the doors into a bright hallway. There is a lot of activity around me. A new doctor is added to my crew. The anesthesiologist. He leans down close to my face, placing his hand on my shoulder, and asks me if I am all right. I'm not, I tell him. Tears again. I didn't get to tell Kira goodbye. I didn't know I wasn't going to see her tonight. I feel like I have no control. I wanted to give her a hug. A kiss. And I hate to be put to sleep. And I'm so cold. I whine like a baby.

But he is good. He asks me if the mask makes me uncomfortable. I tell him yes. He says he won't put it on me until I am almost out. I'll never feel it. (He's right. I didn't.)

I ask him if he is really good at what he does. I tell him that I have read *Coma.*

He assures me that he is one of the best.

I am wheeled into the operating room. Doctor S. comes in. A nurse follows. I ask to meet the assisting physician. I want him to know who I am. So he will care more. I think if he has looked me in the eye, heard my voice, I will be more important to him. I want to be more than just the breast of the day.

And then I sleep.

It's over. My eyes won't stay open. The recovery room is quiet. Two nurses walk by my bed talking softly. A phone rings. My mouth is dry. My tongue feels swollen. It sticks to the roof of my mouth. I want to wake up. I sleep some more.

Someone has placed my hand over my bandaged breast. Did they do this on purpose? So that the first thing I am aware of upon waking is that I still have a breast? I try to keep my eyes open long enough to get the nurse's attention. If she sees that I am awake, maybe she will take me to my room. Michael is waiting.

As my bed is wheeled into the room, I see Michael sitting in a chair in the corner. I am having so much trouble waking up. I want to be clear-headed. I hate the heavy feel of my body. I sleep some more.

Evening. Dinner is brought in. You've got to be kidding. Even Michael doesn't want it. I drift in and out. Irritation is mounting. I want to have a conversation with Michael. But I can't form the words with my mouth. I turn on the television. I think it might wake me up. I don't even know what is on. I drift away again.

At nine-thirty Michael leaves to go home and get some sleep. Kira is spending the night at Becky's. Michael says she had a great day and is doing fine. Just before ten the phone rings. I try to reach it. I can't. It stops. Put the light on for the nurse. Tell her I can't reach the phone. It rings again while she is there. She hands it to me. It's Kira. She is at the climbing gym with Becky and the kids. She wants to hear my voice. To know I am all right. She tells me she loves me. I tell her I will be home tomorrow. I love her. Be good.

Thanks Becky.

I want to get up to pee. Refuse the bedpan. Take it slow, the nurse says. I hurt. Have to drag everything I am connected to along with me. Drainage tubes on my right side, I.V. on my left. We wheel along. I catch a glimpse of myself in the mirror. Wonder if Michael will really come back.

Visitors all night. Checking everything. I am hooked up to a morphine drip. All I have to do is push the button.

At two a.m. a nurse tells me to push it whenever I feel any pain. Everything will heal faster, she says. She tells me that I won't earn any extra feathers for my wings by being in pain. Even in my foggy state I think this is a strange statement. But I push the button.

At three a.m. a nurse shows me a swimming exercise that I can use to rebuild my muscles. At three a.m. . . .

I push the button.

A patient is at the desk outside my door. He is yelling. I imagine that he has a semiautomatic in the pocket of his robe. I can see the headline in the morning paper. The nurses try to calm him down.

Push the button.

The clock on the wall ticks. And ticks. And ticks.

The gentleman in the room next door coughs. And coughs. And coughs.

The woman across the hall moans. Moans loudly. And cries.

Push The Button.

• Wednesday, December 28

Vomit. All morning. Michael comes to see me on his way to work. Can't really have much of a conversation. I have stopped pushing the button and am now coming down off the morphine. My head is throbbing.

Feathers my ass. Where is that nurse now. In the light of day.

Breakfast brought in. Michael eats. I throw up.

Doctor S. stops by. He smiles. Made it off the high dive, he says.

Removed a few lymph nodes. Took out some more tissue. We'll have the results by the end of the week. Go on home.

We do. My mother and step-dad are coming down to stay for a couple of days. They want to help. We can use it. Especially Michael. He has been doing everything. He needs a break.

I sleep. In my own bed. It is early evening when I really begin to wake up. My mother is there. I forget how to be the child. I wish I could remember. It would be easier.

Becky brings Kira home. She lies on the bed with me. I remember how to be the mother.

I sleep.

• Thursday, December 29

I am stiff and sore. But I feel more like myself finally. The morphine must have cleared out. Michael takes off for work. He is able to leave without worrying. He knows my mother will take care of me.

She does. I can hear her fielding phone calls for me. My step-dad entertains Kira. I smell food cooking. Unfortunately I have no appetite. My stomach feels like it has been turned inside out and rubbed with sandpaper. So much for wonder drugs.

A shower is what I want. My hair has that bent look that you get from lying in bed for days at a time. And I smell like medicine.

My right side is covered in bandages from my armpit halfway down my torso. They are thick, rubbery bandages that can handle a bit of water. On the front of my breast, just above the nipple, is an incision about two inches long. It is covered by a clear bandage, looks like plastic wrap. A window for viewing. A small bit of blood surrounds the incision.

I step gingerly into the shower. I let the water beat on my left side. Tilting my head backwards into the steady stream of water, I wash my hair. I am afraid to touch my right side. I save that for another day.

My mother calls into the bathroom to see if I am all right.

I am.

The mirror is completely covered in steam. No reflection. After toweling off I put on one of Michael's old flannel shirts. Button down. Can't pull anything over my head yet.

Kira knocks on the door. She wants to see where they cut me. I let her in. I open the shirt. Just the front. I think all of the bandages on my side would scare her more. The unknown. She looks right at the incision. She looks me in the eye. Does it hurt, she asks. A little, I tell her. But not as much as you might think. Cool, she replies. I am so proud of her bravery. No one else has asked to look.

Off and on I nap. My step-sister and her kids drop in for a visit. I am awake for some of the time.

Flowers are delivered.

The phone rings and rings and rings.

Michael calls. He has just spoken to Doctor S. The cancer was invasive. But the lymph nodes were not involved. They were not asked to participate in the game. Radiation should fix everything.

My mother cries.

• Friday, December 30

My father calls from his house in Oregon. He and his wife go there for Christmas every year to ski. They drive there from their place in Arizona. They are going to cut their trip short and come for a visit. I tell them that's crazy. That I will be fine. My father says that he knows I will be fine. After all I am his daughter. I wonder for a moment if that means he gets the credit for my good health. What if I don't get better. Who gets the blame?

They just want to come for an evening. They'll get a hotel. Don't want to be any trouble. Just want to see me. They'll be here on Monday.

My stepmother gets on the phone. She mentions using visualization. She has read where people can cure themselves. If they think the right thoughts. Meditate. And drink tea.

I have read about this too. But for the first time I see things from this side. Without meaning to, are people implying that if a cure is not achieved, somehow the patient has failed?

Or are people so frightened by this disease that the thought that it can somehow be controlled is comforting to them. Should they ever get it, by doing the right things they could be cured. And when someone they know gets it, they know that anyone can. Even they. And that is powerful.

It will be good to see them. To show them that I really am fine. I really am.

My mother and step-dad pack up to go home. I love them so much for coming. But I feel like I wasn't sick enough. I didn't know how to be waited on enough. I think my mother would have felt better if I could have asked her to do more.

The phone rings. It is the editor of our local paper. I write for them sometimes. He wants to tell me that he will be running one of my pieces on New Year's day. And would I like to be on the Board of Contributors, write for the paper on a regular basis. I can't believe it. A phone call not cancer related. I had almost forgotten about my real life. I am a writer. I write. The editor has reminded me of that. I am so happy.

• Saturday, December 31

New Year's Eve. Our friends Debbie and Felix are going to bring us dinner. Eggplant parmesan and everything to go with it. Even ice cream for dessert. They are on their way to babysit for Debbie's brother so they can't stay.

Becky, Ed and Katy decide to come over and spend the evening. I am hosting a party. And it's catered! Not bad for having had surgery just a few days ago. But I still can't eat much. The food looks great. I eat a turkey pot pie.

We make it till ten-thirty. I'm too tired to ring in the new year. Becky and Ed pack up and take Katy on home. I go in the bathroom to brush my teeth. Michael has promised to stay up till midnight with Kira.

Kira calls me from the kitchen. Tells me there is a present for me in the refrigerator. Brings it to me in the bathroom. It is a small white box. It is tied with a purple ribbon. Gold stars are twisted in the ribbon. A note on the corner of the box reads, Claudia, Happy New Year. Love, Becky, Ed and Katy.

Inside the box is a beautiful silver cuff bracelet. I have looked at this very same bracelet many times. Tried it on, more than once even. But no one knows this. I have never told anyone. I don't know the people in the store. They don't know me. But somehow Becky has picked this to give me. I am stunned. I put it on my right wrist. There is a sun in the center. I wear it so that she is facing me.

The silver shines in the bathroom light. I feel like Wonder Woman.

I call Becky. I ask her what she was thinking. Why the gift. She tells me it is to wear every day of radiation. It is to keep me safe. I tell her I will always wear it. I ask her how she happened to pick it out. She said it just seemed like me.

I fall asleep knowing it will be a very good year.

• Sunday, January 1

We sleep late.

Read the paper.

Admire my article.

Answer the phone.

Go for a short walk.

• Monday, January 2

Michael is still off. I love these three-day weekends. He makes me promise to let my father and his wife stay in a hotel. He knows it goes against my nature.

They arrive late in the afternoon. We just hang out. Watch a movie on television. Order dinner from the pizza place down in the village. A pleasant evening. They see that I am fine. I let them call the hotel and reserve a room for the night.

And I let them go.

I am taking care of myself.

Michael is amazed.

• Tuesday, January 3

Have an appointment with the surgeon today. It has been one week since the surgery. While in the shower I decide to remove the large sticky bandage. I know it has to come off today and I figure it will be easier in the steamy water. It comes right off.

Getting out of the shower I check the mirror. It is covered in mist. I wrap up in a towel and go into the bedroom. I keep my back to the mirror and gingerly dry off. I close the bedroom door. I face the mirror. The incision on the front of my breast I have grown used to. My side, now uncovered, looks as if I have been hit by a bus. I have a large incision under my arm. It is swollen and has black stitches. Beneath it I am covered with dark purple and yellow bruises. I keep remembering how the surgeon told me how great I looked after the surgery. And this is a full week later. And I think I look like shit. Goes to show you the power of perspective.

His work.

My body.

Michael waits in the reception area while the doctor examines me. I think he is afraid to see all that has been done.

The doctor is happy. Takes out my big black stitches. Covers the incision with a narrow strip of adhesive. Says the swelling will go down slowly. He then removes the clear plastic wrap from the smaller incision. I am surprised at how neat it now looks.

I cover myself with the paper gown. He asks if I am interested in a cancer support group. Says there are many wonderful organizations he could put me in touch with. I tell him that I am doing fine on my own. I'm really not on my own. I have Michael. Kira. My family and friends. But thank you. Besides, I don't plan on having cancer much longer. Really, I don't.

He goes to get Michael.

We sit across from the doctor. He says I will need six weeks of radiation. Five days a week. And possibly chemo.

Chemotherapy. This is a surprise. I thought I didn't need that.

We'll have to see, he says. We need to talk to Doctor A. The oncologist. You'll see him on Friday. We'll have more test results by then.

As we get up to leave, Doctor S. puts his hand on Michael's shoulder. Are you doing all right, he wants to know. I know this isn't easy, he tells Michael. There is real concern in his eyes.

His wife has had breast cancer too.

Chemo. It's just a minor setback, Michael says on the way home. We just weren't expecting it.

That night, while trying to fall asleep, I have my first real doubts. I felt so sick in the hospital. And so bad when I first got home. What if I need the chemo.

And what if it makes me sick. And what if I'm not strong enough to deal with it. I find that I am more scared of the treatment than of the cancer.

I dream that we are still living in Mexico. We lived in a beautiful little coastal village an hour south of Cancun. But I am not at the house. I am in the small clinic in the jungle. It is about a ten-minute drive from where we live. I am hooked up to an I.V. and can't leave. I know if I could just get home I would be well. If I could see the water. If I could feel the air. But no one is there to unhook me. And the bed is very high off the ground. I am afraid I will fall if I try to get out.

• Wednesday, January 4

Wake up frustrated and tired.

Have to make a phone call. Have been putting it off. Been working on a children's book and was supposed to meet with the publisher this week. Have to cancel. Not cancel, postpone. Hate that. I have been working on this for so long. Feels like going backwards.

The publisher is completely understanding. I have told her the truth. Her mother went through the same thing last year. Traveled to Scotland for Christmas this year. Not to worry. We will get together when I am ready.

Only another writer can know how awful it feels to cancel a meeting with a publisher.

Michael is at work. The mail has been stacking up. I never sent out my Christmas cards. I have plenty to do to keep busy.

I am amazed by some of the letters I have received. As the word has spread, people have been sending me their generous thoughts.

A parent of one of the children who goes to the school where I used to work writes to me about love and prayer and angels.

An old friend of Michael's, living on the East Coast, writes to say she has a nun saying prayers for me every morning.

My daughter's piano teacher writes to say that "they" must be crazy, saying I need radiation. She says I light up a room by simply entering it. Moon the cancer she says. The letter is addressed to The MIGHTY CLAUDIA.

• Thursday, January 5

I call my friend Pete the Pilot. He used to live in San Francisco and fly for United Airlines. He is retired now and lives up in the mountains of Northern California. We have been friends for twenty years. He loves me and I love him. This is okay with Michael. He understands that you don't come this far along in the world and not find people that you will love forever.

Pete is upset at my news. But he knows that I am just where I need to be. I fill up more pages in Pete's address book than anybody. But for the past eleven years I have been at the same address. With Michael. If that doesn't paint a picture of my life, I don't know what does.

• Friday, January 6

Today I meet Doctor A., my oncologist. Michael has to get to work, so once again Kira is with friends. I owe, I owe, I owe.

The phone rings early. It's Michael's boss, Jimmie. He was diagnosed with cancer almost six years ago. He was given two years to live. He goes to the same oncologist as I do. This is good news. Tells me that Doc A. is a good man. Gives me a pep talk. Tells me I can call him any time. Just to bitch. He'll understand.

If he can walk the walk, so can I.

One couple is ahead of me. Their daughter is with them. She is stunning. Tall, dark-skinned. Looks about mid-twenties. Beautifully dressed. An intricately woven scarf at her neck.

And reading an article about breast cancer.

Her father strokes her arm.

The doctor calls them in.

I never see them leave.

It's my turn.

Get weighed. Undress from the waist up. Put on gown, open down the front. Climb up on table to wait. And wait. Go in search of a *People* magazine. Am becoming fascinated with Charles and Camilla.

Does she sleep over? Are they watched by the Queen? Talk about your Royal pain.

Doc A. comes in. Quiet. Examines my breast. My armpit. Says it looks sore.

Yep.

Get dressed, he says. I'll be back in a minute.

I do. He is.

He opens my folder and shows me all of the information gathered so far. I have cancer. It is invasive. It's not in my nodes. We found it early. He sees no real need for chemo. (Yes!) It would only give me a two-percent edge. There is also an anticancer medication. Can have some nasty side-effects. It too only increases my chance of survival by about two percent. Not interested, I say.

Radiation is the way to go. Five days a week for six weeks would give me the same odds as completely removing my breast.

As long as we are discussing numbers, what are they, I ask.

Eighty-five percent chance of surviving ten years with radiation.

And without radiation, I ask.

Forty percent chance of surviving ten years.

Once again I am stunned at the power of words. He sits calmly, opposite me, looking me in the eye. Forty percent.

I'll have a tuna sandwich.

Nice view.

Come here often?

Words.

We open our mouths and change peoples lives. Or we don't.

Amazing.

I'll take an order of radiation. Hold the chemo. Save my life.

Michael's parents call tonight. Actually they have been calling almost every day. They live three thousand miles away, and this is hard for them. They want to parent us. I know if I asked they would be here on the next flight. But what would be the point? I want them to come in the spring. When I feel new again.

They want to do something though. They want to buy me something to read. My father-in-law reads me the *New York Times* best-seller list over the phone. Tell me what sounds good, he says.

So I do. I am learning something.

When people who love you can't fix what is wrong with you they begin to feel helpless. They really feel better if you let them do something for you. This is important. It isn't about whether or not you need the stuff. It is about the fact that they need to do something. They will sleep better that night. And you may get to read a new book.

Couplehood, by Paul Reiser, was just what I needed to read.

• Saturday, January 7

Becky's husband Ed is a sport. Asks me if I want to go motorcycle riding today.

Yes!

Now Ed's motorcycle isn't one of those little namby-pamby putt-putt kinds.

Ed's is big, and shiny, and fast.

Over the years I have watched with interest as Ed sold one motorcycle to buy another, always getting the latest, most high-tech piece of equipment that could be found.

I would listen with envy as Ed and his friends would plan bike trips to the desert. My mind would wander with them as they spoke of trips up the coast, navigating Highway 1 like a pack of road warriors. I wanted a piece of it.

I'm forty-four. I have cancer. But I knew what I wanted. I wanted one afternoon where I could shake it all off.

So at a bit past noon, Ed roared down my hill and into the driveway. Kira and her friend Erica watched as I put on my borrowed helmet. Michael kissed me good-bye just before I threw my leg over the side of the rocket machine. And we were off.

By the top of the hill I was forty again. Picking up speed on the freeway on-ramp I re-entered my thirties.

Layers were shed. Cancer was left behind.

Little did Ed know, but he was riding with a twenty-year-old college student, known to try just about anything on a whim or a dare.

Now I know all the horrible statistics about motorcycle riding. I would never encourage anyone to start riding. I don't feel the need to have one of my own parked in the driveway. I hope Kira never gets the urge to hop on the back of some crazy kid's bike and rip up and over the hill into the twilight. I really hope she doesn't. But she will be missing something.

She will miss the thrill of flying down the highway at high speed and knowing no fear, only wonder. She will miss the ache in her cheeks from grinning so hard for so long. And coasting. Coasting down a narrow road through the thick forests on Mount Madonna. Sun rippling through the leaves. No sound except the wind as you cut through space and time.

But I didn't miss it. Today I got it all.

• Sunday, January 8

And then there is sex. Or the lack of. It's not that I have forgotten about it. But right now I don't know what it has to do with me. My body doesn't feel like a sexual being anymore. It feels like an obstacle. A problem. Something wounded that needs to be fixed. The enemy.

Also, since being diagnosed with cancer I have had to stop taking hormones. I had been taking them since my hysterectomy seven years ago. To continue taking them would increase my risk of more cancer.

So here we are. Or, where are we?

We are in the land of abstinence. And it isn't a happy place.

And so far I have no solutions. Neither does anyone else. But almost everyone has a suggestion or two. And we are trying them all. I have had to become acquainted with a whole new section of our local pharmacy. The section filled with creams, jellies, lotions. I really think I can only go back there so many times to buy what I feel are very personal products before I will be accused of running a small business on the side. I wonder if they have taken my name off my checks and it now is written on the bathroom wall with the notation, "for a good time call . . . "

So it's Sunday morning and Kira is asleep. The room is still dark. Rain pelting the window. I hear the heater click on in the living room. It is so warm and cozy under the mound of quilts. Michael's arms wrap around me. Careful not to hurt me.

And we try. And we can't.

We've been robbed.

• Monday, January 9

Michael leaves for work early. Kira is still sleeping. I turn on the television. The *Today* show. Katie Couric is ice skating at Rockefeller Plaza. The Christmas tree is gone. Manhattan is just coming to life. I wish I were there.

Every year we go back East to visit Michael's family. Usually at Thanksgiving. They live in New Jersey. Just an easy bus ride away from New York City. And I love Manhattan. We were just there in November. We were at the skating rink. I watched Kira glide beneath the glorious tree that is put up every year. We visited the public library. It must be the most beautiful library in the world. We took Kira to her first Broadway play. It was a perfect day.

Another morning we left Kira with her grandpa. Michael, his brother Bob, their mother, and I went into the city for an adults-only day. We did everything. The Impressionists show at the Metropolitan Museum in Central Park. Some shopping. The taping of the *Jay Leno Show*. (He was in town for the week.) Dinner and a Broadway play.

While walking on the Upper East Side, the light reflecting on the old apartments bordering the park was a soft bronze. The air was cool, but not raw. I wanted to find a bench. And just sit and watch the light change. Watch the people walk hurriedly by. Dressed for New York. I looked up at the apartment where Jackie Kennedy used to live. Where she died.

I could hardly take my eyes off the building.

And then there's the park. Tree limbs bare. But I know they will be full in spring. People riding their bikes on the paths. Roller bladers dodging in and out. Colors flashing. Colors. I love how the cabs are the same golden yellow as the mustard on the hot pretzels sold on almost every corner.

And when I was in New York I wasn't sick. Or at least I didn't know it.

So this morning I wake up early and watch Katie skate. And the people rush by.

And I wish I were there.

• Tuesday, January 10

I am trying not to be small minded. The issue of vanity has come up. Last night I stood in front of the mirror, contemplating my now mismatched breasts. Don't get me wrong, they were never perfect. But now my right breast is one size smaller than my left. I know it shouldn't matter. It is a small imperfection. It is also a small breast. Actually I prefer the new size. But I would like them to match. I feel petty and shallow even mentioning it. So for a while I don't. I mean after all, I am going to live (at least that is my plan), so what is the big deal. But then I look in the mirror.

The truth is, no one would ever notice anything looking at me fully clothed. Unless they really try. But I keep thinking of summer. And my black Speedo bathing suit. It took me years to find just the right suit. It covers me just enough. It feels good in the water. It isn't one of those up-the-butt styles. But it will not be able to hide the fact that one nipple is riding high.

Climbing into bed last night, I complained to Michael. He looked at me as if I were crazy.

They do too match, he argued.

For years I have slept in the buff. For the past few weeks however I have been sleeping in soft cotton T-shirts. I have felt too exposed, too vulnerable, to sleep otherwise.

What, are you blind? I asked.

He put down his book and looked at me again.

Really, he said, they look exactly the same. I can't see any difference.

I can't decide if he is trying to fool me or himself. Or if he simply has no eye for detail.

Look, I say pulling my shirt over my head. Tell me you don't see any difference.

He looks at me carefully. Really looks.

I swear, he says in a sympathetic tone, they look as beautiful as ever. And they look exactly the same.

But his head is tilted at a forty-five-degree angle.

So today I dyed my dark blond hair three shades lighter.

Then it was time to go meet my radiologist. Another Doctor S. He has given me the last appointment of the day so that he may spend as much time with me as necessary.

Do you find yourself wondering how you got in this pickle? he asks.

More a question of how to get out of it, I respond.

That I can help you with, he says.

I like him. He knew my friend who died last fall. We talk about why it happened. Because sometimes life sucks, is his conclusion. He cared about her. He doesn't want to go through that again.

As we sit there in his office, munching on coffee candies, I feel as though he will become a friend. An ally. And he knows his shit.

Driving home in the rain I feel good about all the players on my team.

• Wednesday, January 11

A package arrives from my friend Michele. She and her daughter lived with us a couple of years ago. Now they live in Ohio. Over the past few weeks we have been talking on the phone and writing. We both wish she were closer. She has sent me some special tea. A healing brew. As I hold the steaming mug in my hands, I feel her here with me. Even though she is so far away, she is playing a part in my recovery. And I love her for that.

• Thursday, January 12

I have decided to see a nutritionist. My friends have told me I am too thin. Michael complains about my bony butt. I think there might be something I could be eating to help me get through the radiation treatments with little or no side effects. I also wonder if I might be able to get a handle on this no-hormone thing. So today is my first appointment. In preparation I have had to to write down everything I have eaten for the past four days. That is an eye-opener. I find that when I am writing a lot I forget to eat. I start to make an effort to sit down to a healthy lunch every day. I am loving potatoes. Baked. Sweet. Little new potatoes mashed with butter. I stock up on fresh vegetables. Baby carrots. Artichokes. Broccoli.

My meeting with the doctor goes well. She encourages me to add more exercise to my day. Build up muscle. She is right. I sit at my desk too much.

I also tell her that I have read that drinking miso soup every day during radiation treatments can be beneficial. She agrees. She would like to see me on a regular basis. Monitor what is going on with me.

I make another appointment before leaving the office.

Driving home I have an itchy feeling. I have added one too many people to the team. I know what to do nutritionally. I know I haven't been good about it. I know that I will be now. I feel as though I am giving up any control over my body. There are some things I can't fix, aspects of this challenge that I need others to guide me through. Even to call some of the shots.

But I need to feel capable of feeding myself. And I don't want to be weighed every week. And measured. And I don't want to write down everything I eat. And everything I do. And have to show it to someone and get their approval.

So as good as she is, I cross her off my list. I cancel the next appointment. Because it isn't right for me right now.

And I get some insight about why people with eating disorders have so much trouble getting help. Their problems with food often stem from a search for control. And being put on a maintenance program like this is about giving up your control.

Failure seems to be built in.

• Friday, January 13

A few months ago I watched a special on television about a tightrope walker in France. One of the best in the world.

A vineyard out in the countryside was celebrating an anniversary.

This vineyard, heavy with grapes, is located in a small valley. At one end of the valley stands a castle. Centuries old. Casting shadows over the lush land. Directly across from where the castle stands, at the far side of the vineyards, is the road leading to the village.

The road is hugging the top of a ridge. Making it the same height as the castle turrets.

The owner of the vineyard has decided to throw a party. The entire village is invited. Many of the members of the community work in his vineyards—some for generations.

Food is ordered. The best wine is set aside. And as the crowning touch, the world-famous tightrope walker is hired.

A massive cable is strung across the valley, from one of the castle turrets to the road leading into the village. A distance of over a mile. A height of at least one hundred feet.

Days are spent checking the cable. Watching the winds. Planning a walk that looks to be impossible.

Or at least unlikely.

And then the day arrives. Music is playing. Hundreds of people have turned out for the event. Children are running among the arthritic vines, bending with the weight of yet-to-be harvested grapes. A foggy mist hovers over the valley. The cable is slick with moisture.

The master-walker checks the wind. He climbs over the top of the stone turret. He tests the cable. He steps out, holding one of those long poles for balance. And he starts his walk.

Below him the people watch in frozen silence. No one wants to see him fail.

At one point the wind picks up. The cable bounces with the force of it. So he sits. Waiting out the weather. Not wanting to fall.

And when it seems safe, he continues his walk. At one point, feeling confident, he kneels down and balancing on one shoulder does a complete somersault.

And again continues walking. No one can help him. They can only watch, necks crooked, eyes fastened to this lonely figure in the sky. A bird on the wire.

But only he can do it. And it doesn't mean he's a hero. He isn't superhuman. He simply knows that once he has set out on this journey, he needs to finish it. By keeping his eyes on the horizon. Never looking down. And placing one foot in front of the other.

He does it.

And boy do they party.

Sometimes at night, when I can't sleep, I think of him.

• Saturday, January 14

Tomorrow is Kira's friend Erica's birthday. Erica's mom Nora has invited Kira to spend the night. She doesn't know how much Michael and I appreciate having some time alone. To just let down. And it is so good for Kira to be somewhere else. Where the phone isn't always ringing. Where she doesn't have to listen to the latest cancer update.

So I rent a movie and we fix some dinner and settle in on the couch.

Later we half-way succeed at sex. It is as good as a weekend away.

Thank you Nora.

• SUNDAY, JANUARY 15

We invite some friends in for football and pizza. The house is filled with children. Big, hairy men are staring at the television screen as though the outcome of the game may really affect their lives. Pistachio nuts are falling down between the couch cushions. Rings are forming on the coffee table. Beer bottles are piling up in the kitchen. Becky and I leave the chaos for an hour and hit an after-Christmas clearance sale.

And when we get back I eat two pieces of pizza.

And drink a chilled glass of Fumé Blanc.

How good life can be.

• Monday, January 16

I am proud of myself. Every month I write for a local women's paper. This month I owed them a book review and a first-person piece. I read the book. I wrote the review. I completed the column. I met my deadline.

I'm saving this issue.

Went to a birthday breakfast this morning. A good friend is turning forty-something. There were five of us sitting around the table. Pots of tea at each elbow, covered in cute little cozies.

Two of the women I haven't seen in weeks. But I am sure they know what has been going on with me.

So we make small talk for about an hour. Our kids. School. Work. Movies. Brad Pitt.

We eat hot, buttery popovers. We get refills on tea. Cards are opened.

But there is an undercurrent.

I look at my watch and see that now almost two hours have passed. I need to go. I start to gather up my things. Settle the bill.

And then someone asks. How are you really? What are the doctors saying?

The table seems to shrink. All eyes are on me. Four women. Women who appear frightened. I feel as though I have crossed over into another dimension. They want to know what it is like.

They're standing on the bank of a lake and watching me plunge in to the murky green water. As I rise to the surface they can't help but ask.

Is it cold?

How does it feel?

Not really wanting to go in and find out for themselves.

Well it is cold.

And it's dark.

But while underwater, if I open my eyes and look up, I can still see the sun.

• Tuesday, January 17

Big day for doctoring. Appointment at the hospital for a scan. Get a clear picture of where my heart and lungs are located before we start radiation. Then on to the surgeon.

One of those days where I can't escape. But I will be fine.

I ask a lot of questions. The machines, the technology, are really very interesting.

But it is a long afternoon. Kira has gone to a friend's after school. By the time I get there to pick her up I am emotionally drained. I have hit the wall.

After dinner I can't find Michael. We only have a few rooms in the house, and he isn't in any of them. I open the door from the kitchen to the garage. He is sitting in the Trooper, doors closed, blasting Jethro Tull on the tape player.

He too has hit the wall.

• Wednesday, January 18

I've lost track of the moon. I don't know if it is full, quarter, or just a sliver as it comes up over the redwoods in our backyard. I keep forgetting to look.

• Thursday, January 19

A doctor-free day. After Kira leaves for school I go back to bed. I sleep for two hours. I take a bubble bath. I put Melissa Etheridge on the stereo. Loud. And I go out into the garage, leaving the door to the kitchen open so I can hear the music. I put on my boxing gloves. My bright red boxing gloves. And I start to punch the bag. It's a small punching bag, but just right for my healing upper body. And I punch. Hard. Harder. I dance while I punch. A crazy bird-like dance. And I sing along. In a barking kind of voice. Like a gull searching for the sea.

And I open the garage door. I don't care who sees.

• Friday, January 20

I am lying on a table in the radiologist's office. Right breast exposed. Two lab techs are marking me with deep purple ink. I am told not to move at all. We are mapping for radiation.

The techs leave the room. One of them speaks to me from the observation area.

"Hold your breath."

I do.

A screen is to my left. Film has been loaded into it. A light is positioned on my right. My breast is silhouetted on the screen. It looks like a small hill. It has a gentle slope. I imagine soft green grass. Spring. I am lying on my back in the grass. I am staring at the blue, cloudless sky. A breeze tickles the hair on my bare arms.

I hear Kira's laugh. It floats to me. I sit up. Kira and Michael are running up the side of the hill. A kite snaps over their heads. It dips. But doesn't fall. They run faster, toward me. They tumble in a tangled pile at my feet. Laughing. Out of breath.

The sun is warm on my face. I can taste it.

"Now breathe."

The lab techs are finished.

It's time to go home. It hurts to shift the gears.

And it's raining.

• SATURDAY, JANUARY 21

I'm out of here. Last week I read in the morning paper that three of my favorite writers were going to participate in a fund-raiser in San Francisco. I called Becky to see if she was interested. She was. So I called the number listed and snagged two tickets. Listening to three writers whom I really admire read bits and pieces of their work seemed like the perfect way to spend an evening. The wine and snacks were an added bonus.

We decide to make a day of it. Becky picked me up about ten a.m. I read her some of what I've been working on while we drive to the city. She likes it. Plus I like that now she knows how I'm really feeling.

It's a rainy day. But that doesn't matter. We hit an outlet or two. I buy a birthday present for Kira. We have lunch at a favorite Italian place just off Union Square.

It feels wonderful to be wearing "city clothes" instead of sweats and leggings. Clothes that have to be dry cleaned. Real shoes with hard soles. Makeup. I feel better than I have in days.

By the time we arrive at the house in the Castro neighborhood where the event is to take place I have almost forgotten that there is anything wrong with me.

And I love this house. An old two-story Victorian at the top of a hill. Filled with interesting artwork. Colorful people. Views of the Bay from more than one window. Downstairs a cellist is playing. Upstairs a classical guitarist makes graceful background music. Conversation flows. So does the wine.

I need to use the bathroom. The old clawfoot tub is filled with ice. Wine bottles are stuck in the ice at cheerful angles. I check my reflection in the mirror. I look like my old self.

It is time for the authors to read.

I join Becky. Somehow we have become stuck in a corner. She can just see over the people in front of her. I can't. And there is nowhere to move. We are jammed in.

A couple is just behind me. A tall couple. Seeing my dilemma, they grab a folding chair from where it was stashed behind a desk. Stand on this, they tell me. I refuse. I'll look stupid. I'll block their view. No really, they insist, climb on up. We can still see. You'll never see a thing if you don't. I look around again. They're right. And I have come a long way.

So I climb on up. The gentleman holds the chair steady, only letting go when he sees that I'm okay.

I survey the crowd. I am heads above everyone. One of the writers looks up at me and smiles. I give a small wave and smile back.

And I am not embarrassed.

Perched there. Like an exotic bird.

Out on a limb.

• Sunday, January 22

Today I blew it. Thought I'd been doing well at keeping it all together, but guess not.

Been remembering to pick Kira up from school. Take her to piano on Mondays. Hebrew school on Wednesdays. Birthday parties, etc. But I lost it today. I delivered her to the temple an hour and a half late for Hebrew school. Didn't even realize it. The new time was on the school calendar, but I never looked. So I just pulled into the parking lot and dropped her off. As I was driving out, I noticed that the lot was full and no other kids were being dropped. Odd.

By the time I arrived home I was convinced something was up. Got out the calendar. Saw that class had started at nine-thirty instead of eleven. And that it was over in twenty minutes. Just time enough to go back and get her. Swell.

Kira hates to do anything wrong. Doesn't like to stand out in a crowd. I know that she will be an absolute wreck when I get there to pick her up. She is probably panicked that I won't even get there for another hour and a half. She'll be stuck. Waiting at the front door. Watching the rain.

I curse myself all the way there. Ready to do anything to make it up to her.

I am a bad mother.

Pull in the parking lot and find a space. I dodge raindrops and run inside. The kids are still in class.

There is a large sign on the bulletin board informing parents of the special class time. I haven't been to temple for a few weeks, so I missed it. No excuse.

Here she comes. With her friend Rachel. She's laughing. We walk out to the car and I start to apologize.

No sweat, Mom, she says.

Did you worry if I would be back on time, I ask.

If you didn't I'd just call you, is her wise reply. I keep money with me, she adds.

Climbing into the car she looks over at me.

Cool, she laughs, only a half hour of school today. Think Dad will want to go roller-blading?

Sure. Why not.

Cool.

• Monday, January 23

It's the first day of radiation treatments. I am prepared. This is to help me get well. It doesn't take very long. I know that I will sail through this. And in six weeks it will be over.

Piece of cake.

I have my own cubby next to the dressing room. It has my name on it. My own gown is in there waiting for me to put it on. The sight of my name on the cubby bothers me. Makes me feel like I am a member of some club I had no intention of joining.

I step into the dressing room and take off my shirt. My bra. The purple marks have faded a lot. I have been told that I may not use any soap, lotion, or deodorant on the side of my body they will be irradiating. I haven't been. But I get night sweats. I find the purple ink on my sheets in the morning.

I start to blame myself. But then change my mind. They need better ink.

Leaving the dressing room, I place my things in my cubby. No, not my cubby, the cubby. I take a seat. Look at a magazine.

They are running a bit late, I am told. Just a few more minutes. I read an article about the French Impressionists show I went to in New York last fall.

My turn.

I am led into a room with a narrow table. Climb on up, I am told. My knees are positioned. My gown is slipped off of my right side. My head and arm are put into position. The lab tech asks if I am all right.

Yes, fine, I tell her.

Good. Don't move. This is a bit more complicated than we thought. You have a misshapen right lung. We will be irradiating more of it than we want. But don't worry. If something develops later on, you still have plenty of good lung left. Okay, hold still. That's perfect. I'll be right back. Breathe easy.

And I'm alone.

But just for a second.

Women come quietly into the room. Maybe a dozen of them. They are wearing flowing gowns. Gauzy. Spring-like colors. They have wreaths of herbs and flowers in their hair. They are carrying candles. Their faces are floating in the soft light. They make a circle around me and begin to chant a haunting incantation. I feel the warmth of their bodies. They come in closer. Closer. Performing their magic healing.

I close my eyes.

There. All done. Wasn't so bad, says the tech.

No. Not really.

You know, you could try some visualization if you want too, she suggests.

Maybe so. Maybe so.

Get dressed. Check the mirror. My neck is splotchy. Red. I sit for a moment. Start to leave. Feel queasy. Get into the small bathroom. Vomit. Wash my face. Rinse my mouth. Find a lemon candy in my coat pocket. Suck on it slowly.

Make small talk with a woman on my way out the door.

Get in the car and head out on the freeway to pick up Kira at school. Cry for three exits.

• Tuesday, January 24

I'm still surprised at my reaction to yesterday. But I'm beginning to understand it.

For the most part I don't spend much time thinking about cancer. I think about what to cook. What project I am working on. If I want to walk the dog or not. When the rain might stop. Kira. Michael. Not cancer. And that works for me.

But then there you are. In a gown. On the table. Machines aimed at your breast. Lines on your body. Everyone else leaving the room. And it's like a cold slap in the face. You've got it. At least for now. And that scares the shit out of me.

But today will be easier.

Tomorrow even better.

And it is. I cry for only two freeway exits. And I don't lose my lunch.

A friend calls to see how I am feeling. Was today easier. Did I throw up again.

She tells me that twice in her life she has thrown up and embarrassed herself greatly.

Once on a plane. Into a total stranger's lap.

Another time while trying to perform oral sex.

But at least she knew him.

• Wednesday, January 25

I am noticing something about going to my radiation treatment. My appointment is at nine forty-five every morning. Some mornings it is as late as nine-fifteen before I step into the shower. Am I in denial? I really don't seem to remember that I am going until about nine o'clock. Then it's a mad scramble. I drag into the doctor's office right at nine forty-five.

I am usually early everywhere else.

Maybe this means something.

Kira has Hebrew school today at three-thirty. I'm taking her. I get to school just before three to pick her up. Plan on having her show me what she has been doing in the classroom.

Find a parking place. Get my jacket from the back of the car to put on. It's raining. Lock up.

I love the yard at Kira's school. A narrow path winds past the younger kids' classrooms. Lawn is on each side of the path. A few years ago a fund-raiser was held. For twenty-five dollars you could have a personalized brick made. A brick with your child's name. Your family name. Whatever. The bricks were placed in the path.

Every day, when I walk down the path to Kira's classroom, I read the names of the children on the bricks. And I picture their faces.

I read Kira's name.

And I am so glad this is where she spends her day.

Zap.

While driving home I make a mental list.

1. Learn more about classical music.

2. Find out what it is about opera that people love. Learn the stories. Listen to the music. Develop a favorite.

3. Discover a new writer.

4. Really learn to box.

A friend of mine calls on her lunch break. I haven't spoken to her since just after my surgery. I really didn't think much of it. But she is calling to apologize. She starts to cry.

Seems she has been thinking of me a lot. But when she thinks about me, and what I have, it scares her. She tells me that she is afraid that I am going to get sicker. That I might die.

So she's started to pull away. Thinks it will lessen her grief. Thinks that if she gets used to not seeing me now, she won't miss me so much when I am actually gone.

But she feels guilty. So she called.

And she's crying.

Takes guts to be this honest. I tell her. I tell her that maybe other people feel the way she does. But she is the only one who had the balls to tell me.

And I'm not mad at her. I feel bad for her because I know this will bother her a lot longer than it will bother me.

Plus I tell her that if I were dying I would want her to feel free to be as honest with me as she wanted. Tell me if she is scared. If she hates this. But *talk* to me. So that if she were to wake up at night and not be able to go back to sleep, she could replay one of our conversations in her head. Not lie there and think of all the things left unsaid.

But I'm not going to die. If she had just asked me I could have told her.

• FRIDAY, JANUARY 27

Super Bowl Frenzy has hit everywhere.

I check into radiation and all of the lab techs are wearing football sweatshirts and have black chalk lines under their eyes.

Forty-Niner raccoons.

Big sugar cookies are sitting out on the table. They are covered with red frosting. Outlined in chocolate. A white "SF" is scrawled in the center.

I'm sure bets are being taken somewhere on the premises.

Goes to show you, you never know what parties you might be missing by being in the wrong place at the wrong time.

Helped myself to two cookies before leaving.

By the time I got home, Kira's teacher had called. Kira is sick. Could I come and get her.

As I pull into the school parking lot and get out of the car I am surprised at how tired I have become. Really tired.

By the time I get to her classroom I am in a cold sweat.

There she is. Isolated from the rest of the kids.

She gathers her stuff together and we head back to the car. It is raining again, but I don't have the energy to button my coat.

Have to stop at the grocery store on the way home. I know once we get home I can't go back out unless I leave Kira home alone. Don't want to do that.

So we walk the aisles. And fill the cart. And wait in line.

Kira can see how lousy I feel. She unloads the groceries at the check stand and goes in search of a loaf of French bread for dinner.

When we get home she unloads all the bags of groceries from the car. Places each one on the kitchen table. Asking me all the while if I am all right.

By the time we get the food put away it's pouring outside.

So we curl up in bed together. Under the quilts.

And rest. So we both can get better.

The rain won't stop. It just keeps hammering. At three o'clock we lose power. The sky is so dark that we need to light candles. Kira loves this. We find every candle in the house, light them, and place them on the mantle in front of the mirror. I build a fire in the fireplace. We settle in on the couch with books and listen to the storm. I open the sliding door to the backyard so we can hear the creek rushing down below our house.

Michael gets home from work and we eat in front of the fireplace.

I doze a bit on the couch, wrapped in a heavy quilt.

Kira has mouthed off to Michael. He's calm with her, but she keeps trying to get the last word. She's digging in. No graceful way out of this one.

I watch and listen from my nest on the couch.

Michael refuses to lose his patience. She finally sees his point. They talk about the issue of respect. Soon they're both laughing.

Michael taught Kira to ride a bike. To skate. Every night before she goes to sleep they play games together. Geography games. Math games. Brain Quest. Every evening he sits with her while she practices piano.

She has inherited his love of sports. They sit up late at night to watch hockey on television. If Michael can't get home to watch, she watches it alone, and tells him what he missed.

For years people have told me that Kira is just like me.

I have always argued that point. She's Michael, I'd tell them. You're just fooled by her blonde hair. Her blue eyes.

Tonight, while they talk, I don't say anything to either of them. It's almost as though I'm watching from outside. Through the window. It's as though I'm not even here.

And I know, for the first time since she was born, that Kira and Michael would be fine. If ever I weren't here.

• SATURDAY, JANUARY 28

I'm so tired again today. And depressed.
Could be the weather.

We still have no power.

And I have no power.

• Sunday, January 29

Michael is going to the store. He asks me what I want. I have no appetite. No interest in food. Or cooking. I don't care what he buys. Get what ever you and Kira want. Get vegetables. Fruit.
I don't care.

And then I think of something.

Yellow chrysanthemums. A potted plant. They have them at the grocery store. At the back, by the dairy section. I can see it on our dining room table. A bright chunk of color. It has been raining so long. Everything is so gray. Forget food. This is what I want.

I can hear him in the kitchen getting ready to leave. I call out to him. Come here, I thought of something.

He has his list in his hand. Toilet paper at the top of the list. We ran out. Sunday morning with no toilet paper.

He looks at me expectantly.

A yellow chrysanthemum. With lots of fat flowers.

Before I can finish my request, his eyes have rolled back in his head.

That's all I needed. I'm pissed.

He leaves. Comes back with everything, even the flowers.

And I am still pissed. So is he.

We yell. Kira is outside. She comes in and tells us to stop. She accuses us of planning a divorce. Lots of her friends' parents have. She takes my side, seeing me as the weaker one right now.

So we stop. And I try to explain my need for the flowers. My need for a spot of color in the dark living room. How just looking at them will make me better. Better than a new jar of peanut butter. Or chicken. Or green apples. And that if I weren't so tired I would go to the store myself. And get my own flowers. And this wouldn't be an issue.

And that I hate this.

But I understand Michael. He's tired. He is doing more than his share. And he's worried. So to him flowers seem like an unnecessary detail in his day. A stupid thing to think about.

And he hates this too.

So today is a hard day. And I'm feeling dark. And sad. And overwhelmed.

The phone rings. It is my ex-husband. I haven't spoken to him in years. He and his wife, whom I have never met, live hours from here. Seems they have been at a party all day. Watching football. And drinking. Someone, a mutual friend, tells him that I have cancer. So he decides to call.

Michael hands me the phone. A strange look on his face.

Hello.

Hey Pal. Do you know who this is?

I would know this voice anywhere. I mean, I was married to the guy. And I know exactly what has happened. It's a Sunday. There's a big game on. He loves football. Loves to drink with his friends while watching the game. Makes bad decisions while under the influence.

I can hear his wife in the background. He's calling his ex-wife, she is telling someone loudly. There is astonishment in her voice.

So, did you like the game? I ask. Have any money on it?

No response. The reality of what he has done has hit.

A friend takes the phone from him. Apologizes for the call. Says he never saw a party break up so fast. Wives are packing up their husbands and taking them home. It was just that my "ex" was concerned.

Tell him I'll be fine.

Tell him I'm not angry. Not about anything. Life's too short.

I hang up the phone.

Michael and Kira are watching me. No sense in even trying to explain this one.

Later, in bed, I feel so much better. My life has moved on. Today I got a phone call from the past. And my ex-husband still seems to be living in those dark days.

And I'm not.

So who's the lucky one.

• Monday, January 30

Starting to feel like I might not be able to do this on my own. I may need to look into a support group. I keep telling myself that the worst is over. The end of all of this is in sight. But it doesn't feel that way. It feels as though I am shrinking. And it is growing larger all the time.

Like a huge dark cloud on the horizon. And I have to make my way through it. Once on the other side, the sun will be out again. But for now it is just getting darker and darker. And cold.

And I feel alone.

Today is Michael's birthday. I feel like I am cheating him out of something. He deserves better than this.

I'm sorry, Michael.

• Tuesday, January 31

I need help. This is too much for me today. Maybe it is like after being in a horrible car accident, and finding that you really will be all right, there is a sense of relief. But then you see your totaled car. A mass of twisted metal and broken glass. Your knees buckle. You get sick to your stomach. And you can't stop shaking. You know that you will be fine, but the thought of how it could have turned out is overwhelming. All you have to do is look at the car.

And all I have to do is look at the scars.

I hate cancer.

Even when this part is over, I will always be afraid of it coming back. And that isn't fair.

I'm not as tough as I thought I was.

And I just want to cry.

• Wednesday, February 1

I am on the freeway heading to the radiation lab for my morning zap. The sun is out for the first time in weeks. I close my eyes for just a second. The Trooper is replaced by a motorcycle.

I wish I didn't have to wear a helmet. I lift the plastic face shield. Feel the wind on my skin. It makes my eyes water. But that's different than tears. I hear the roar of the engine.

I'm singing songs in my head.

I get off at my exit. Weaving around cars moving too slow for my taste. I'm not in a hurry. Just don't like to waste time. Not on a sunny day.

The parking lot is half empty. I cruise through it looking for a space. Then change my mind.

As I ride up to the front doors of the office, they both open automatically, leaving just enough space for me to ride on through.

I have never ridden a motorcycle down a flight of stairs.

It is easier than I would have guessed.

The lab techs look surprised to see me.

The noise of the idling engine fills the small waiting room.

I shut off the motor and put down the kickstand.

My leathers make a soft creaking noise as I dismount. I take off my helmet and put it under my arm. Approaching the cubbies I notice that they are small. My helmet will never fit in one

The thin cotton gown that I wear every day is stuffed into the cubby. Waiting for me.

Reach for it, but change my mind.

My boots echo loudly as I walk down the hall to the radiation room.

Entering the room, I place my helmet on the counter where I usually stash my purse.

Climbing up on to the table, I unzip my jacket. Pull my right arm out of the sleeve, exposing my right breast. Purple ink marks, tattoos. Biker-bad-ass.

I lie back on the table. Right arm under my head. The lab techs adjust the machine.

They zap.

They zap again.

And I sit up and zip.

I put on my helmet.

Wave goodbye.

Riding up the stairs is easy.

The doors open.

I roar down the driveway and out onto the busy street.

I can feel the warmth of the unexpected winter sun through my black leather jacket.

Break the three-digit speed barrier on the freeway heading home.

• THURSDAY, FEBRUARY 2

Went with my friend Nora to the doctor's this afternoon. She has a small lump in her breast. She is very frightened.

Maybe I can ask questions that she hasn't thought of. Maybe I can drive her home if the doctor tells her something that frightens her even more.

Odd to be at the doctor's and not be the patient. Nice for a change. But not for Nora.

They call Nora in. I go with her.

Shirt off. Gown on. Open down the front.

Here, wear my Wonder Woman bracelet. It helps. Really.

Nora places the silver cuff on her right wrist.

Doctor comes in and introduces himself. Places films of Nora's mammogram on the screen.

Doesn't see anything.

Feels the lump.

Cyst, he says. I think it's just a cyst.

If it doesn't go away after your next period, we could aspirate it. See what's in it.

Nora doesn't look happy about this suggestion.

Waiting that long is asking a lot.

Does she have to wait? I ask.

No. I could do it today.

Do it today, Nora says.

And he does. And it's clear. The liquid is clear. Which means he's certain that it is a cyst. A harmless cyst.

Yay Nora!

After getting dressed again, she returns my bracelet.

I put it back on, glad for its protection.

And we drive home in the warm late-afternoon sun.

• Friday, February 3

Two weeks of radiation finished. Four weeks go.

Sat in the car for a few minutes this morning before going in to treatment. Watched the people come and go.

Something is really wrong with this picture.

It is a spectacular day. Low seventies already. The sky is a blue that artists dream of.

The ocean is calm. Deep azure. Purple kelp beds floating on the surface.

The surrounding hills a soft velvety green.

Pink blossoms on the cherry trees alongside the driveway.

And people going in and out. In and out.

For radiation.

For now anyway, making it a part of their day.

Something is wrong.

• Saturday, February 4

So the other night I'm feeling guilty about not making very interesting dinners lately. It's stupid, I know. But I can't help it.

Reheat some spaghetti from a couple of nights ago.

Dish it up.

Dinner's ready, I call.

Michael and Kira sit down at the table.

Cool, Mom. Pasta Déjà Vu.

Good attitude.

Last night, before getting into bed, I felt something strange. Like an electrical force traveling around my legs.

I stood in the hall and tested it. Yep, if I brought my legs close together, but didn't let them touch, I could feel it. It kind of tickled. My two calves were almost touching and no mistake, I could feel something.

I climbed into bed with Michael.

Listen, I told him. I'm radioactive. I can feel it. There is some kind of force surrounding me. When I put my legs close together, but don't let them touch, it kind of tickles. In a prickly way.

Get out of here.

No, really.

Come on.

No really. I'll turn on the light.

So I do. And I look.

At five weeks worth of leg hair.

And still Michael kisses me goodnight.

• Sunday, February 5

Yesterday my sister Carol and her friend Toni Ann came by with a picnic lunch for me.

Last week my sister Cheryl sent me super vitamins.

Sisters. Very special people.

Went motorcycle riding with Ed again today.

I trust him completely. Even at high speeds.

But there is this one pass. He knows which one.

I tell him later. I am surviving cancer. I also want to live through the ride home from San Juan Bautista.

But it was great. And I felt so good.

Get in to bed tired at the end of the day. Curl up next to Michael. He places his hand over my right breast and holds it.

Like a small bird with a broken wing.

• Monday, February 6

My mother called last night. She feels helpless. She wishes she were closer. I wish she were too. So she could check on me every day. So I could check on her.

Going to go to my first support group tonight. Have mixed feelings. Would skip it with the slightest encouragement.

But then I think I would regret not going. And I would rather go to bed tonight knowing I had given it a shot, even if it's not for me, than go to bed wondering what I had missed.

• Tuesday, February 7

Didn't go last night. Do wonder what I missed.

By the time I got home from Kira's piano lesson I was exhausted. Went to bed by seven o'clock. Not like I could sleep or anything, but just couldn't be up any longer.

So I just rested and listened to the house noises.

Michael fixing dinner.

Hockey on television.

Piano practice.

Bath water running.

And I wrapped up in my quilted cocoon and settled in for the night. And dreamt of spring. And flying.

• WEDNESDAY, FEBRUARY 8

I grew up in the fifties. Back when girls had to wear dresses or skirts to school.

I would walk to the grammar school every day. Shirtwaist dress. Plaid pleated skirt. Little pastel-colored blouses with Peter Pan collars.

What I wore never determined how I spent my time in the school yard, however.

Knees were skinned. Dresses torn and stained. It didn't matter.

Now don't get me wrong. I was no athlete, but that wasn't the fault of my clothes.

I just never felt secure up at bat.

Felt short on the basketball court.

Hated being hit playing dodgeball.

But I loved the bars. It felt wonderful making my way to the top of the climbing structure. Straddling it. Checking out the view.

A large sandbox sat off to one side in the play yard. Three different sets of bars sat in about two inches of pea gravel.

This was where I could be found hanging out at recess. Literally.

My favorite was the bar that stood about four feet off the ground.

I loved the feel of its cool smoothness as I slapped my hands over the top of it. I loved the strength of my arms as I pulled myself up, throwing one bare leg over the top and hooking on.

And then the push off. Keeping a firm enough grip on the bar to keep from falling. But leaving enough space between my palm and the cool metal to allow me to spin.

One second I would be looking at the gray pea gravel, the next the sky. Voices blended together into one constant back ground noise, punctuated by a shout or scream as a point was scored or a tag made.

And I would spin. Counting. How many times could I throw myself over? Pull myself up. Every day trying to beat my own record.

My skirt would fly behind me. Underwear was something everyone was used to seeing in the yard.

Spinning. Gray ground. Blue sky. Flashing colors in between.

Gray.

Blue.

Gray.

Blue.

Until I could spin no more.

Then I would throw my other leg over the top of the bar. And drop down. Releasing my hands. And simply hang. Skirt falling over my face, making a small tent around me.

My hands dragging through the gravel.
Making designs.

Sifting. Pouring.

Feeling sheltered from the outside world. Voices muffled by the skirt of my dress. By layers of petticoats.

But there was a price to pay for all this joy.

The burn on the back of my knees. Bar burn, we called it. And it hurt. Not unlike the radiation burn that I am beginning to feel these days. Tight red skin.

But I wore those burns proudly. Like a badge of strength. I had earned them.

They proved I could go the distance.

That I could spin and spin and spin.

• Thursday, February 9

Had a visit with my doctor after my radiation today. He told me he wants to extend my treatments one more week. That means that tomorrow isn't the halfway point after all.

Now I know that this is really for my own good. That it is no big deal. It's just one more week. Five treatments. Insurance.

But it stinks.

And I get in the car telling myself that something good had better happen today. To balance things out. Or I'm gonna cry "no fair."

I get home and there's a valentine on my gate. A homemade valentine. Red construction paper. White lacy heart. And in the center a sticker with a little pink Cupid. Inside the card is a tiny pocket. Stuffed in the pocket are two candy hearts.

No name on the card. No signature.

But I'm sure that it's for me.

• Friday, February 10

She comes in just after I do every day. About my age. Athletic looking. Sweatpants. Sweatshirts. Rubber flip-flops. Like she's on her way to the beach for a walk.

Some days she comes for chemo.

This past Monday she complained of nausea for the first time.

Tuesday she leaned against the wall for just a moment after treatment.

Wednesday I noticed a shuffle in her step.

Thursday she wore slippers instead of her rubber sandals.

Today her husband held her elbow as she left.

Fuck cancer.

So swell. Michael shaved his beard off today. I loved his beard. It looked great on him. And it helped hide the fact that I'm nine years older than he is.

Thanks to lack of hormones I'm in the middle of menopause and feeling really old while my husband looks about twenty-five.

So this is the picture. I feel like crap. Tired. Hot flashes. An uninspired (and I'm sure uninspiring) sex partner. My husband has never looked better.

Ironic, huh?

I asked him why.

Just needed a change.

Me too.

I really should be in writing class today. Learning, not teaching.

Adair Lara is teaching a class today in Marin County. I try not to miss any of her classes. She writes for the *San Francisco Chronicle*. She is one of the reasons I take the paper.

It's always worth the two-hour drive up. I come home energized. Inspired.

But I had to pass on this class. Timing isn't what it should be.

So I'm lying in bed and imagining what's going on.

For starters, Adair is visibly upset that I'm not there. She looks over the crowd, hoping to see my face. Wondering if she should even bother teaching a class that I'm not in. What would be the point?

She thinks about calling writer Anne Lamott. Another of my teachers. Maybe Anne would know why I'm not there. If there is a good reason why I didn't sign up for the workshop. Something she said. Or didn't say.

Leaving thirty students waiting, she goes in search of a phone.

"Anne, Claudia didn't show for my class today."

"You know, she hasn't dropped in on my Wednesday night class for ages either. I've been starting to lose interest in teaching. But you know, all these other people signed up. So what could I do?"

"Exactly. I mean I'm sure these people in the class today are perfectly nice, but they're no Claudia."

"Takes all the fun out of it, huh?"

"Exactly."

"Adair, you don't suppose she found another teacher. Someone she thinks is better than you—or me."

"I did hear she took a class with Isabel Allende."

"I ran into Isabel. It was all she could talk about."

"Oh god. Maybe that's it. I gotta get back to my class. I just don't know how I'm gonna show any enthusiasm for teaching today."

"Hang in there. We'll get to the bottom of this. Whatever we've done, there must be a way to make it up to her."

"What ever it takes. I'll do it."

So Adair teaches the class. She uses some of my work as examples of how to put words together to create beauty.

And on her drive back to The City she brushes away a tear.

• Sunday, February 12

Woke up about three a.m. and couldn't fall back to sleep. Couldn't get a picture out of my mind.

Imagining one of my doctors telling me they were sorry. It was unexpected. But the cancer is back.

Know this isn't healthy. Isn't wise. What if just thinking about it makes it more likely to happen.

But it's hard. Once it has happened, it's easy to imagine it happening again. Impossible not to think about. No matter what you tell yourself.

Like being at a small party. Eight or ten people. And off in one corner of the room is a ten-foot kangaroo. Standing by the fireplace. Roasting marshmallows.

Enjoy yourself, the host invites. Have a glass of wine.

Mingle.

But please. What ever you do. Don't mention the kangaroo.

Don't look at him.

Don't talk to him.

We like to pretend he simply doesn't exist.

If we give him attention, it only encourages him.

Oh, I can do that. Sure.

Except that there are mirrors on every wall. And everywhere I look I see ten-foot kangaroos, with marshmallow dripping down into their big furry pouches.

• Monday, February 13

Years ago I used to do volunteer work at San Quentin Prison. Sat on a committee.

Once or twice a month I would visit the prison and attend meetings there. Meetings that could only be held there. To accommodate the inmates who also served on the committee.

It usually took around an hour to get into the prison. Past checkpoints and guards. Then we might meet for an hour or so. By three or three-thirty we would have to call it a day.

Lock-down was at four.

It got to where every day at four o'clock I would think about the men in San Quentin. That they were being locked in their cells once again. It wasn't that I wanted them out. Or that I was particularly sad about their situation. Most of them were there for good reason.

It was simply that now I could put names and faces to many of them.

And at four o'clock every day I could imagine what was taking place in their world.

Even when I no longer went to meetings. After my work at the prison was done, four o'clock still haunted me.

Sometimes it still does.

Every day at nine forty-five I go for radiation.

And I wonder how long it will be before that time of day means nothing.

• Tuesday, February 14

Valentines Day. Heart-shaped cookies served up with a dose of radiation.

A small white box, tied with red ribbon, left on the hood of my car. No note.

Layers of red and white tissue paper stuffed inside the box.

In the center of the tissue, a small golden cherub.

Blowing a kiss.

Making a wish.

The moon is full tonight.

• Wednesday, February 15

The sun is out. I get work done.
The dog gets a bath.

I am halfway through my treatments.

• Thursday, February 16

Met a woman at treatment today. The machines were down, so we all had to wait. More and more women coming in. Filling chairs. Filling the normally quiet room with conversation.

This is her second round. Seven years ago she had breast cancer. Now it's back. With a vengeance.

She has completed chemo. It did no good.

This is her last day of radiation. It doesn't seem to be doing the trick either.

Her doctors have told her she may as well decide how she would like to spend the time she has left.

They're speaking of weeks, not years.

She says she might travel. Go someplace warm.

Let the natural radiation from the sun take its shot.

She's not angry.

But her husband is.

He's not ready to give up his best friend.

It's her turn to see the doctor.

Then my turn for treatment. The machine is now working.

When I finish she's gone. I know that I will most likely never see her again. If for no other reason then that her treatments are over.

But I think about her.

She has beautiful dark brown eyes.

And a nice smile.

She loves the ocean. Being outdoors.

She likes Champagne.

And to laugh.

I wish I had hugged her.

• Friday, February 17

False summer. But I'll take it.

After treatment Kira and I meet up with friends and head down to the beach. No school today. Presidents' Weekend.

Stacks of driftwood cover the beach. Natural hideouts created by the winter storms.

Kira and her friend go claim their fort. We don't see them for at least an hour.

The Bay is empty. Too early in the season for boats to be brought in and tied to their buoys.

I close my eyes and dig my toes in the pebbly sand.

I can see the sun through my eyelids.

A little girl's voice bounces off the driftwood piles. It stings my ears.

She's screaming.

I sit up and open my eyes.

She's spinning in circles in the wet gray sand. Footprints chasing her. Arms flying overhead. Terror in her cries.

I look over at my friend. She seems to be sleeping. Hasn't heard the small girl's screams.

I get up and leave our blanket. Head toward the child.

I can't see what has frightened her so. Early bees? Sand fleas?

Her back is to me as I approach.

Get it off me, she cries. Get it off me! Get it off me!

She is brushing away something invisible.

Spinning around, she looks up. Eyes wide. Tears streaming.

And I look her in the face.

And it's me.

• Saturday, February 18

Sunlight pouring through the window. Patterns on the bed and wall.

But I'm sick. Might be the flu.

Close the curtains.

Sleep all day.

• Sunday, February 19

Better today. Becky has a surprise for me. A gift certificate for a facial. A day of makeovers at her house.

Pam is having her hair colored. Her eyebrows. And lashes.

Becky is getting a trim and condition.

And I'm getting my face smoothed and plumped.

Three women from Marin County are coming to spend the day making us beautiful.

We sit around Becky's kitchen surrounded by food and fashion magazines.

The beauty experts from Marin look us over.

I am very aware of my "trim-it-myself" haircut. And my straight-from-the-package color.

Hair looks pretty good, they agree.

Color is nice.

But you need eyebrows. Yours are almost invisible, they say.

Makes you look stunned. You don't want to walk around looking stunned all of the time.

So darken the eyebrows I tell them. We'll see if that does the trick.

But I have a suspicion that wiping the stunned look off of my face isn't going to be that easy.

• Monday, February 20

No radiation today. Holiday weekend. I'm glad. My skin is really beginning to itch. That sunburn kind of itch that hurts to scratch. So I'll take a day off from treatment where I can get it.

My mom and her husband come down from the Bay Area for a couple of hours.

They think I look good.

I do too.

It's the eyebrows.

• Tuesday, February 21

They ran late at radiation today. Pisses me off. I have a life to get on with. Bad enough I have to come here every morning. They could try harder to be on time.

Know that I'm being unreasonable.

But who am I supposed to be angry at?

So I'll just have to be mad at "THEM."

Have a meeting with the editor of our local paper this morning. Been hoping to get some steady work. Something I can count on, rather than just running a column once in a while.

I am right on time.

I'm taken to his office.

Take a seat. He's not there.

Hear him come down the hall.

He's tall. Has a nice smile. And a messy desk.

We spend an hour talking. Getting to know each other. He has given me a column. Only once a month. I rotate space with other writers.

But on a regular basis, it will be my space. With my name. My picture. In the Sunday edition.

For everyone to read while eating bagels in bed and drinking cups of strong black coffee.

And no one got me this job. No one put in a good word for me. And it has nothing to do with my having cancer. No one felt sorry for me and decided to give me this to make me feel better.

I got it because I am a good writer.

And I can even write that and leave it in.

• Wednesday, February 22

The bills are piling up. Medical bills.

Michael has been wonderful. He's been assuming all responsibility for keeping them in order. Filing claims. Showing me where to sign.

I asked him to. Told him right from the beginning that I didn't think I could cope with them.

It's not the paperwork so much, although I am slightly allergic to paperwork. It's just the act of opening the mail every day and reading about cancer, and where it is in my body.

But for some reason today I opened the mail.

"Infiltrating Duct Carcinoma and Intracystic Papillary Carcinoma of the right breast."

And I started to shake.

The power of words.

• Thursday, February 23

Today I see the doctor after my treatment.

Something happened to me last week that bothered me so much I couldn't even write about it until today.

Once a week I see the doctor who has prescribed the radiation treatment that I receive. This treatment is what is supposed to be saving my life.

I was measured. Tattooed. Marked. Scanned. X-rayed.

So that we could all be sure that this treatment would work for me. I have put my faith in those measurements. In those who did the measuring and in the doctor reading those measurements.

And every day I lie there and expose myself to radiation. I believe that this doctor knows exactly what I need to have done. And he is doing just that. We're talking trust here.

So last week as I sat across from my doctor, wearing my flimsy cotton gown, he asked me, Why did you get implants in the first place?

What?

Implants. Why did you get them?

Before he can finish asking his question for a second time he is opening my chart. A flush is creeping up his neck.

I don't have implants.

I'm sorry. Of course you don't. I was thinking of someone else.

I'm sorry.

Thinking of someone else.

While it's my turn. *My* six minutes. My weekly exam.

And I am so ashamed at my reaction to his huge mistake.

I told him it was okay. I gave him an excuse. He sees so many people. I let him off the hook.

I don't tell him how completely let down I feel. How my faith is shaken. That there is no excuse for what he has done. That the very least a doctor can do is check the chart of the next patient before entering the examination room to make sure who it is and what they have. Make them feel that at least for those six minutes they are the most important person in the world.

Instead I laugh it off.

And all week I can't decide who I am angrier at, myself or him.

So today when I see him I tell him how much last week bothered me. That I need to know that he knows who I am.

Again he apologizes. It will never happen again.

I believe him. But something has been lost.

That sense of security derived from knowing that you are the most important person in the world for six minutes, once a week.

• Friday, February 24

Food. My friends have started bringing us food.

A few weeks ago my friend Lindsey asked me if she could organize dinners for me. Friends of mine had asked her if I would like that. Could I use the help?

At the time I still had most of my energy so I told her not yet. But I would let her know when.

Last week I saw Lindsey at school picking up kids. And she came over to my car to talk.

We talked about the kids. The weather. Small stuff.

And as she started to leave I stopped her.

About those dinners. Could we start now? Maybe twice a week?

I could tell she knew it was hard for me to ask.

I have a whole list of people just waiting, she said.

And she did.

Lasagna. Chili. Roast chicken. Salads. Teriyaki chicken. Chicken soup. My favorite artichoke jalapeño dip—with chips, wine.

Once again I wonder how I could have done this alone.

• Saturday, February 25

Flu-like symptoms once again. Guess this is the pattern. Radiation buildup.

One doctor told me that it is to be expected. Another says it shouldn't happen.

The lab techs say it happens all the time.

One opinion is that these treatments are harder on larger people. They need higher doses of radiation to penetrate the denser tissue.

Another is that it is tougher on smaller people, like myself.

Science.

So I drag myself down to the video store and rent three foreign films for the weekend.

The sun has been gone for a week. No regrets about not being outside.

I call Nora. She lives right next door.

Wanna do nothing with me for a couple of hours? I ask. I rented some movies. I'll bring one over if you're interested.

Sure.

So we curl up on her couch and ignore the gray weather. Reading subtitles. Eating cookies.

Later that night I tuck up against Michael in bed and listen to the owl in the redwood grove just beyond our back fence.

The hollow, lonely sound he makes is perfect to fall asleep to.

• Sunday, February 26

Not so fluish today. Just tired.

Michael has gone on a bike ride up the coast with a friend.

I can picture where they are. I wish I were with them. Even though I could never keep up. Not even on a good day. But it would be wonderful riding along, watching the curve of the coastline, the waves breaking over the outcropping of rocks.

I take Kira to Hebrew school. She's going home with a friend afterward. Then Michael and I have a date.

After his ride, and a shower, he takes me downtown to one of my favorite bookstores for a browse. The browse turns into a buy.

Then a late lunch and a movie.

I sit as close to him a possible in the darkened theater. My arm wrapped through his.

We share a box of M&Ms as we watch a movie that turns out to be much sadder than either of us had anticipated.

We both cry.

And I realize that this is one of the reasons I married Michael.

Because he can cry at the movies.

• Monday, February 27

If it's Monday, it must be fryday.

After today only nine more treatments.
The countdown has started.

I've been listening to opera. I love it. Becoming a real opera-head.

Yesterday I bought a book with the stories behind some of the most famous ones.

I've started preparing Michael. Dust off that tie.
Next season, we will be attending. At least once.
Probably the cheap seats.

And he promises me he'll go. And he always keeps his promises.

Saw a poster with my name on it today.

I've been invited to read at a benefit on March 10.
A fund-raiser for a women's cancer support group.

I love that it comes right at the end of my treatments.

It's a sign.

• TUESDAY FEBRUARY 28

Stretched out on the table. One of the lab techs calls for the doctor. Seems they need to draw new lines on my breast. Starting Thursday they will be homing in on the exact place where the cancer first started growing.

The lion's den. The dragon's cave.
The monster's closet.

I close my eyes and wait for the doc.

I hear a soft, swooshing sound. And gentle footsteps.

My head is turned to the side. I open my eyes and look down at the floor.

Red boots. And blue tights. Red trunks. Blue jersey with a large red "S" placed in the center of a yellow triangle.

And the cape. Draped over his shoulders. The exact same shade as his trunks.

He's shorter than I would have thought. Has a slight potbelly. I don't remember the mustache. And he's still wearing the Clark Kent glasses.

He takes the cap off the pen. Looks carefully at my breast.

Using his x-ray vision, he makes his marks.
The purple marks.

The bulls-eye.

Perfect, he says.

And I have to believe him.

I mean, come on.

Lois always does.

• Wednesday, March 1

It's supposed to rain this afternoon. But it hasn't started yet.

Got home from treatment today and let Moka in the house. Tail wagging.

A patch of sun was falling on the floor in front of the sliding glass door. Moka claimed it for himself.

It looked good to me too. So I joined him.

My thick, grey, flea-infested fur pillow.

Outside I could see the blossoms on our plum tree, over in the corner of the yard.

Delicate pink blossoms promising sweet dark fruit this summer.

And I imagine sitting under the tree. Biting into the first plum of the season. Juice trickling down my chin. Down my wrist.

And I know that no plum will ever measure up to that first one.

But just to be sure I'll try another.

And another.

And another.

There was a new woman today. A new name on a cubby close to mine.

She sat in the chair next to me.

Staring straight ahead.

Without my realizing it, the torch has been passed.

I'm now the old pro.

She doesn't look ready to talk. Maybe tomorrow.

And then I can tell her.

Don't be afraid. You can do this.

Yes. You can.

• Thursday, March 2

Time to pick up Kira at school.

At the entrance to the yard some kids have set up a table. They are selling tickets to their class play.

Eight-year-old Dylan asks if I want to buy any.

I can't, I answer. Kira has a birthday party to go to that same night. But thank you for asking.

That's okay. So, how's your breast?

A dozen freckled faces look up at me. Not one giggle over the "b" word.

Getting better, I tell him. Getting better.

Been thinking about my friend a lot. The one who died of breast cancer last fall.

They say by the time a lump is found, the cancer has been there for awhile. That means the last time I saw her, I most likely had it.

We sat in her bedroom together talking about her daughter. Her past. Her life. And how neither one of us wanted it to be over.

And I was able to tell her how much I admired her.

For years she had been a single parent. Working fulltime and with the help of her father, taking care of a young daughter.

Then he had become ill, and she cared for him until his death.

And she did it all with grace.

So we sat in her sunny room, and I told her how much I thought of her. And how unfair this all was.

She was angry at the thought of not being at her daughter's Bat Mitzvah next year.

I still held out hope that she would.

And she sat there in bed. Propped up by pillows. Translucent skin hugging delicate bones. No hair. And no scarves or hats or wigs to hide the fact.

Her hands rested on top of the blankets. Pale as the cotton sheets.

Every now and then her eyes closed and she drifted off. Then they would flutter open and she would smile and apologize.

Before leaving that day I put some homemade turkey soup in the refrigerator. Bread on the counter.

I believed the soup would do the trick. Believed it.

Standing out in her yard I tried not to cry.

The sun was hot on my back. Indian summer. Leaves crunched under my feet as I walked to my car.

I wanted her to be well and I felt guilty that I was.

And all that time, my own cancer was growing.

And if we had known that, while sitting in her room on that early fall afternoon, maybe it would have helped.

To know that I was standing on the same side of the river with her.

• Friday, March 3

Today was the first day of my booster treatment. Took a little longer than usual and burned a bit more.

Good thing the women in the lab are so pleasant.

They really are. Always quick with a joke.

Kind of like being treated by Larry, Moe and Curly Joe.

• Saturday, March 4

Kira spent the night at Katy's house. It's another rainy day, so Michael and I decide to take in another movie. I could get used to this.

• Sunday, March 5

Michael makes coffee and brings in the morning papers. I have a column in the Santa Cruz paper today. They're running a new picture of me with this one. I like it better.

Kira and Michael are going to the school skate-a-thon today.

Wish I had the energy.

I spend the whole day reading and napping.

Gearing up for my last week.

Is it really almost over?

• Monday, March 6

Went to a cancer support group this evening and as I sat there and listened to women tell their stories, I realized that it won't ever be over. Not really.

On December 23rd, when I sat on my couch, phone to my ear, and listened to my doctor tell me that I have cancer, my life took a turn. And I can never go back to the way things were. I'm traveling a new road.

So I'm looking for the lesson.

I believe that we learn from every experience we have. If we are paying attention.

One night, early on in my diagnosis, Michael said how unfair he thought this all was.

He said he knew how much I loved my life. That I could see how green the grass is after the rain. Hear the magic in Kira's piano playing. Appreciate the taste of a well-made margarita.

I didn't need a wakeup call.

He's right to an extent.

I look out my window in the morning and get lost in the view.

I see the fog come in off the ocean and really do imagine soft grey cats.

I can spend time sitting at my computer and my mind will wander off to the first time Michael kissed me. The flowered skirt I was wearing. His hand on the curve of my hip. The moonlight coming through the window into the darkened room.

I can remember it exactly.

When he comes home at the end of the day, I still feel the same.

The creak of our porch swing makes me smile.

Watching Kira sleep at night I know there is a God.

I have never asked, "Why me?"

More to the point, why not me?

I don't think I caused my cancer. I don't think anyone causes their cancer.

Like earthquakes, or finally having your acne clear up, it happens.

So I'm looking for the lesson. The epiphany.

And I think I'm getting closer.

• Tuesday, March 7

Woke up in the middle of the night afraid. I have been depending on the radiation to keep my cancer at bay. Like spraying the garden with weedkiller. We stop spraying soon. And then it will be up to me to keep watch. Constantly checking for suspicious little green shoots.

• Wednesday, March 8

Came home after radiation and took a nap. Then went up to San Francisco to see *The Phantom of the Opera.* Got the tickets seven months ago. Great seats.

Don't care how tired I feel. Not gonna miss it.

Becky, Ed, Katy, Michael, Kira and I.

Pouring down rain. High winds. Dinner out. Frontrow seats. Throw up in the women's bathroom. Incredible performance by the understudy. Kids sleep like curled up sow bugs all the way home.

Worth it.

• THURSDAY, MARCH 9

My last day of radiation. The lab techs have a surprise for me. *Phantom of The Opera* plays while I am zapped. They give me stickers and candy when we are finished. It's difficult to say good-bye.

Drive home in the rain. Heading up the hill to my house I get such a sense of coming home. Like Dorothy after she clicked her heels.

Pull in the driveway. The house is quiet, dark. It's pouring out.

I have been looking forward to this day for weeks. Been wanting to do something. Been wanting to wash off the purple lines. Erase the maps and drawings showing the path of the cancer.

I want to feel clean.

So I go into the bathroom and turn on the shower. It drowns out the sound of the rain. Stepping in I can just see out the window up high over my head. It is as wet outside as in the shower.

I turn off the water.

Grab my towel.

Dance drippingly through the living room. Pause for just a second at the sliding glass.

Tall trees. High fences.

Open the door.

My feet are cold in the wet grass. The rain is plastering my short hair to my head. I throw the towel onto the porch. I don't care if it gets wet.

I lather up. Slippery soap slithering over goose-bumped breasts.

I look up at the heavy sky and let the rain rinse me off.

Bubbles form in the puddles around my feet.

Grab my towel and dash inside. I have never been cleaner.

I crank up the wall heater and dry off.

Stare at my reflection in the mirror. Faint purple lines. Scars. Radiation-burned skin. Misshapen breast. At first glance, ugly.

But I keep staring. And see more.
I see a healing woman.

With scars that will fade. Skin that will mend.

She is beautiful.

And seeing this is so unexpected.

Like discovering the rainbow of colors.

In the feather of a crow.

Epilogue

It's been almost a year since I was diagnosed with breast cancer. As I glanced at my kitchen calendar the other morning, already filling up with plans and commitments, the date seemed to jump out at me. That square seemed larger than any of the others on the page. The number seemed to pulsate.

Last spring, after navigating the holidays, wet weather, surgery, and two months of daily radiation, I was tired. I felt depleted. Vulnerable. I noticed I felt more comfortable curled up in bed with a book, or watching television, than visiting with people. I no longer knew the art of making small talk.

After the rainy season finally ended, Kira's class at school began organizing its spring camping trip to Yosemite. Michael volunteered to go along. They would be gone a week. I could spend some time by myself. They could spend some time away from me. We would all benefit.

Unbelievably, I had never been to Yosemite. I was born and raised in Northern California, but somehow never made the trip. The images of the crowds always put me off. Camping has never been one of my favorite pastimes. But at the end of the week, when they got home with their stories and their rolls of film, I was envious.

Call the Wawona, said Michael. Get us a reservation for a long weekend. You'll love it.

The first available weekend was in five months. I grabbed it. Put it on the calendar. Went on about my business.

Our Yosemite weekend finally arrived. We packed up the car. Dropped Kira off at Katy's house. Took Moka to the kennel, and we were off.

This was our first weekend alone since I got sick. We didn't even turn on the radio. We talked. We gazed out the windows. We stopped for coffee and scones. It didn't matter where we were going or if we ever got there. It was simply grand to be on the road.

I watched as the landscape changed from valley to foothills. I smelled the pines as we climbed in elevation. We wound along the Merced River. A lone fisherman stood under the shade of an oak, casting his line. As we entered the park, I was amazed at the fall colors. The reds and yellows of the dogwoods and birch. The indigo sky. And around the bend, the cool granite of El Capitan.

I was beginning to get it.

Wait, Michael kept telling me. There's more.

We drove through the valley and back out again heading toward Wawona. A sign on the left read: Glacier Point, 16 miles. We turned off and drove through the woods. The air was crisp as fall apples.

I was unprepared. Nothing anyone could have said would have been adequate. As we came around the corner, there it was. Half Dome.

We pulled off the road and parked. There was a small clearing and an outcropping of rocks. Michael and I climbed out onto the smooth granite ledge. I sat down and leaned back. It was so beautiful I had to remind myself to breathe.

The sun was shining on the back side of the dome, highlighting the smooth, round curve. The face was in shadow, accentuating its cold, flat surface.

The valley lay before us. The deep gouge where the glacier cut its path was just to the left. But my gaze kept returning to the huge granite monument. As the sun rotated, light began to pour over the sheared-off portion of the dome, exposing the crevices. The web of scars. Imperfections that add to the beauty. That tells a story.

I leaned back against Michael and experienced a perfect moment in time.

After everything—floods, storms, avalanches and glaciers—Half Dome is still here.

And so am I.

About the Author

A columnist for the *Santa Cruz County Sentinel* in Santa Cruz, California, Claudia Sternbach is mother of Kira, wife of Michael, and primary caretaker of Moka the Wonderdog. She has been published in *Redbook* magazine, the *San Francisco Chronicle*, the *Chicago Tribune*, and two anthologies: *In Celebration of the Muse* (Quarry West, 1996) and *Storming Heaven's Gate* (Plume, 1997).

Colophon

This book was designed using Stone Sans as the text type, Optima as the head type and Carmella Handscript on the cover.

Interior stock is 50% post consumer recycled 55# high-bulk cream offset. The cover stock is 80# coated with velvet varnish.

Book design by Tracy Lamb.
Cover photo by Tracy Lamb

About Whiteaker Press

***The truth of our lives—
the power of our stories.***

Whiteaker Press is a Seattle-based group of women writers and designers who believe in the transformative power of the written word.

We are dedicated to producing beautiful books that combine outstanding literary content with design excellence.

Giving voice to those who have gone too long unheard, we bring you stories of creative discovery, spiritual quests, feminist insights, lesbian/gay experience and more.

Also from Whiteaker Press

Stealing Fire
by Claudia Mauro
ISBN 0-9653800-0-9

Animal Tails: Poetry & Art by Children
by Shelley Tucker, Ph.D.
ISBN 0-9653800-2-5

Openings: Quotations on Spirituality in Everyday Life
by Shelley Tucker, Ph.D.
ISBN 0-9653800-1-7

Reading the River
by Claudia Mauro
ISBN 0-9653800-3-3

204 First Avenue South, Studio 3
Seattle, Washington 98104
1-800-489-9095
Email: cmauro1@aol.com